"Let the words of a Poet be forever engraved in the hearts of those who dream, for their eyes will adorn a new freedom, as the music plays on."
- Kenny Lord

THE BELLS
OF HUMILITY
Poetry For All People

KENNY LORD

authorHOUSE®

AuthorHouse™ LLC
1663 Liberty Drive
Bloomington, IN 47403
www.authorhouse.com
Phone: 1-800-839-8640

Published by AuthorHouse 03/12/2014

ISBN: 978-1-4918-7259-8 (sc)
ISBN: 978-1-4918-7258-1 (e)

Library of Congress Control Number: 2014904921

Author—Kenny Lord

Also Author of, "On Faith We Fly"—Poetry By Nature—
Published 2013 by Authorhouse.

Contents

This book is dedicated to those that have the courage, integrity and love, to defend the weak, be a voice for those that cannot speak and to help those in a time of need, when they are unable to help themselves.

To our brothers keepers.

Preface

*T*hroughout my adversities in life, I have always remained resilient in my quest to get by. From the moment my 16 year old mother gave birth to me, I believe that I developed an instinct from her, to ride the rough waters and make it to the shores of dignity, pride and self-worth. Every child deserves to get the chance to walk these words of personal freedom. Unfortunately, many do not. I did. I faced the many and I paid the piper. I graduated from high school, 3 Colleges, instructed at 2 Colleges and I am a very proud Police Officer with the Toronto Police Service. I beat the odds.

I have often wondered how worse things could have been for me. I have seen it firsthand. I have seen the social problems, the drug addicts, alcoholics, the ones held in incarceration, the disabled and the many others that are caught up in unfortunate circumstances, some who really never had a chance. I feel it most for the ones that were born into a privileged life and then it all went down from there. The ones that had the power and the means to help the less fortunate and didn't. The ones who forget that we really are our brother's keeper and who could have been born into poverty instead of privilege.

Hence, "The Bells of Humility".

Every time I take up a pen to write, I feel a freedom like no other. My words, my feelings, my expressions, my poetry. It's like a review of your life that you think about, with a kind sense of, 'wish I could have done things differently' and 'glad I ventured down that path'. Of course, as always, my poetry is mixed with dreams and fiction, my always self-esteem inflator. For my start was a very confused, hurtful one that took years of different experiences and good people to keep the ship afloat. I remember everyone on my life's team and am so grateful to them. I show my appreciation by doing and giving the same kindness to others.

Humility is a part of life's vocabulary that maintains grace within. It admires simple life and wears the robes of freedom for all. And at the sounding of the "Bells of Humility", we will seek to overcome the sometimes overlook and find the strength to rise to the occasion. It is for those times that we pray for.

For the ones that were, thanks for being in my corner. The bells sounding and because of you, I'm still standing.

A Diamond Sky

MY DEAR HUSBAND
UP WITH THE GODS OF FOREVER,
TODAY I HAD ANOTHER ASK ME FOR THE GIFT OF MARRIAGE
BUT AS I LOOK AT THIS STARRY NIGHT OF BEAUTY
I SEE ONLY YOU
I SEE YOUR SMILE
I KNOW LOVE IS ALWAYS TRUE
I FEEL YOUR THOUGHTS ON MY PLEASURED MIND
I FEEL YOUR WHISPERING WARM BREATH
I SEE OUR LOVE THAT WE CARVED FROM BEGINNING
UNTIL YOUR END,
I SEE SOMETHING THAT I NEVER WANT TO SHARE
WITH ANYONE ELSE,
SINCE WE TOOK OUR MARRIAGE VOWS,
NOT EVEN WITH WHAT THE KIND WINDS
HAVE BLOWN ACROSS MY PATH
AND I REMEMBER US,

I REMEMBER THE SOFT TOUCH OF YOUR HAND
WARM AGAINST MY CHEEK, WITH MY EYES CLOSED,
I REMEMBER EVERY OF YOUR WORDS,
THAT SEEMED SO PERFECT,
AND I FEEL THE PULSE OF YOUR HEART,
WHICH THEY SAY IS GONE,
BUT I FEEL IT STILL, BREATHING LIFE INTO ME,
AND SO ON THIS EVENING TO YOU
WHILE WE BOTH SPEAK IN SILENCE
AS MY TEARS FALL DOWN MY FACE THAT
YOU ONCE KISSED MANY TIMES,
I KNOW YOU ASKED ME TO BE HAPPY BEFORE YOUR PASS
BUT HEAR MY WORDS, I CRY TO YOU,
NEVER COULD I SHARE MY LIFE
WITH ANOTHER, EXCEPT FOR YOU,
SO TODAY I RECONFIRM MY OATH
FOREVER TO ALWAYS BE TRUE,
FOR LOVES COMES ONLY ONCE UPON A TIME,
SO I WILL WAIT FOR YOU MY LOVE
TILL ONCE AGAIN
I AM YOURS AND YOU ARE MINE.

A Seas Treasure

SEA TURTLES SHELL,
BRITANIAS BELL
A PEARL UPON HER THRONE,
A SEAGULL WATCHING OVER ME
AND A DOLPHIN TO BRING ME HOME,

THE TROPIC BREEZE
ON SUNSET SEAS
AS CORAL BLOOM THE BLUE,
AN ANCHOR SLEEPS THE SANDY BAR
A MERMAID CALLS TO YOU,

AND WHEN I SURF
THE WAVES TO STILL
AS I WIPE THE SPRAYS OF TEARS,
MY EYES ARE CAST UPON THE MAST
WHILE I SAIL TOWARD THE YEARS.

Bay Leaves

SCENTING BUSY MINT, WITH WAYS OF PRECIOUS GOWNS
IT CAME TO ME,
THAT WHAT I VALUE MOST
WHILE MERE MORTALS CLAW FOR FLEETS THAT BOAST,
IS MY WAYS THAT I AM
THROUGH THINGS THAT I CAN,
ANCIENT PASSING GIFTS,
TRAVELLED IN LOVE,
FOR TO BE GRACED,
TIS FAIR TO SURRENDER OUR THANKS
FOR WHAT WE POSESS LEAST OF,
THROUGH COMPASSION.

Blue Ribbon

*N*EVER FORGOTTEN
MANY VOICES FOR YOU,
COURAGEOUS AS WE SEARCH
TO SEE OUR JOURNEY THROUGH.

Broken Shells

UPON THE SOFT LEAVES AND TWIGS YOU LAY
ABANDONED,
PIECES OF A NEW KIND OF WORLD
SCATTERED THOUGHTS
FROM THOSE THAT FAUGHT,
NOW PEACE AFTER THE STORM
BEHOLD A LIFE OR THREE IS BORN,
AND WARMED BENEATH A MOTHERS FEET
NOW FEEDING HOPE FROM TINY BEAK,
THE CHIRPS THAT BREAK THE MORNING DEW
A CHORUS FROM THE CHOSEN FEW,
WITH EYES THAT BARELY BREAK TO
SEE THE MORNING GLARE
AND LITTLE HEADS AFLOAT,
STILL NOTE AFTER NOTE,
FROM THAT SAFETY NEST UP HIGH
THE CROWDS OF NATURE
CELEBRATE THEIR BIRTH
AND AWAIT THEIR FREEDOM FLIGHT.

Courageous Truth

WHEN YOU DISCOVER AS YOU DRIFT
WHAT YOU THOUGHT YOU KNEW BUT DON'T,
WHEN YOU BEGIN TO SEE THE WORLD
AS CLEAR AS OTHERS WON'T,
WHEN PAIN BECOMES TOO MUCH TO SMILE
AND YOU FEEL LIKE YOUR ALONE,
THEN CLOSE YOUR EYES AND START AGAIN
REMEMBER WHEN YOU WERE HOME,
THERE ALWAYS COMES A TIME MY CHILD
TO SEE THE STORM PASS THROUGH,
AND HOW YOU STAND THE TEST OF IT
IS STANDING ME WITH YOU

Crown Jewel

A KITTY YOU SAY
AS YOU WATCH ME AT PLAY,
AS I BRAVELY GO
I'M A LION YOU SHOULD KNOW,
I SLEEP WITH ONE EYE
AS I WATCH ALL THE LAND,
MY MAINE IS THE SIGN
OF JUST WHO I AM,
THE BIGGER THE ZOO
IF YOU GO THERE TO SEE,
IS THE BIGGER I AM
THAT SURELY IS ME,
A CIRCUS IN TOWN
WHEN THEY ALL HERE MY ROAR,
THEY SURELY WILL STAND
AS I COME THROUGH THE DOOR,
THE STRENGTH OF A LION
YOU CAN READ IN A BOOK,
FOR ALL TO ADMIRE
AS THEY FIGHT FOR A LOOK,
ON TOP OF THE MOUNTAIN
THAT'S WHERE I WILL STAND,
A POWERFUL RULER
WATCHING OVER MY LAND
SO WHEN YOU WALK IN A FOREST
REMEMBER ONE THING,
FOR IT HAS BEEN WRITTEN
IN THE JUNGLE IM KING.

Dancing The Blue

SHE DANCED IN THE SUNLIGHT AND
SHOWED HER AMAZE,
THE POWER WHILE FIGHTING
TO STAY,
SHE SHOOK HER HEAD BOLDLY WHILE
FIGHTING THE HOOK
AS UNDER SHE WENT FOR A PLAY,
SHE RAN FOR THE SEAS THAT WERE
OPEN TO QUEST
AS SHE SPLASHED AND TURNED OUT
TO HER SIDE,
BUT OUT ON THE BANKS AND FOR
THIS I GIVE THANKS
THERE REALLY IS NO WHERE TO HIDE,

NOW HOURS HAVE PAST AS SHE
NEVER GIVES UP
AND MOVES WITH THE WIND AND
A NOTE,
FOR SURELY SHES TACTIC,
AND READY TO RUN
AS SHE TRIES TO OUT DO THE BOAT,
SHES CLOSE TO THE STERN AND ITS
ONE FINAL DIVE
AS SHE SHAKES HER HEAD WITH HER
SWORD,
HER COLOURS ARE CLOSER,
THIS BEAUTIFUL BLUE
THE WINNER IS MARLIN ON BOARD

Flying With Angels

HARPS THAT PLAY ON FLOATING CLOUDS
THE MANY STRINGS THAT GRACE THE HOUR,
TIS ENDLESS SOUNDS ONCE CAUGHT IN BLISS
SHALL MAKE A STUMP SEEM LIKE A TOWER

AS ALL AT ONCE A ROLL OF STRINGS
ARE CAUGHT IN CHARMS WITH ANGELS WINGS,
AND MAKE NO SOUND TILL SLEEP HAS DRAWN
AS OFF IN CLOUDS, IN PEACE TILL DAWN,

SO PLAY THE SONGS OF ANCIENT STILL
MY BEATING HEART WILL MARK,
COMPLETE MY LOVE WITH SONGS OF GLEE
PULL SOFTLY, STRINGS OF HARP

Gifts In The Garden

ONE BY ONE, THEY GROW
SOME FASTER, SOME SLOW,
IT IS THE HEART OF LOVE
THE SOIL HAS COME TO KNOW,
AND AS I WAITED
THROUGH THAT BIRNHAM WOOD CALL,
MY THOUGHTS RUMBLE
IN THE QUAKE OF IT ALL,
MINDS THAT STRAY, SMALL WORK, MORE PLAY
AND OFTEN HAD THE INTENSE GALL,
THROUGH TAUGHT AND LOVE I CAME TO SEE
ONE BY ONE THEY RETURNED TO ME,
WITH OPEN ARMS AND MINDS AS THE PAST TO BURN
WE ALL HAD FATE, TO LIVE AND LEARN.

Grown In The Sun

I LIVED AS A BOY TILL I STARTED TO LEARN
WHAT REALLY MAKES YOU A MAN,
ITS NOT THE SHAVES
AND LATER DAYS
BUT BEING THE BEST YOU CAN,
I USED TO BE TALK WITHOUT ANY DEED
SO NOTHING GREW UP IN MY MIND,
ALTHOUGH I WAS TALL,
WITH SUITS AND ALL
THE KNOWLEDGE I STILL HAD TO FIND,
MY LOVES AND MY LOSSES AND PEERS AND MY BOSSES
AND LIVING WITH FAILURES BEGAN,
TILL TIME STOOD STILL
WITH A WANT AND A WILL,
I STARTED BECOMING A MAN.

Highlands Piper

I WILL WALK IN SOMBER SILENCE, BAG IN HAND
WHILE BRAVE STAND BOLD AND FORAGE TILT,
THE STILL WIND HUDDLES TO A BEAT
MY TARTAN PRIDE WILL WEAR MY KILT,
SOON THE TUNES OF PIPES BLOW SWEET
THE VALLEYS DEEP AND MOUNTAINS HILLY,
ECHOED YEARS FROM WHEN THEY CAME
THE SILENCE BROKE BY MARCHING GHILLIES,
FOR SOLDGIERS PARTED TO THE DAY
OUR THOUGHTS TO GOD AS BAG PIPES PLAY,
THE TUNES OF HONOUR BEG OUR TRUTH
WHILE ON OUR HEARTS WE NOW REDEEM,
FOR GOD AND COUNTRY REST THIS SOUL
UPON THE FIELDS OF SCOTLANDS GREEN.

Hold My Hand

THIS LIFE WE BUILD
THIS HOME WE LIVE,
OUR LOVE WE SHARE
OUR FAITH TO GIVE,

THE ROAD AHEAD
LEADS TO A PLACE,
WHERE RIVERS RUN
BY GODS OWN GRACE,

COME WALK WITH ME
MY HEART I SEND,
AND BE MY LOVE
TILL TIME DOES END.

Holidays And Snowy Days

WHEN THE HOLLY GLOWS AND THE SNOW LANDS SOFT
AND CHESTNUTS FILL THE AIR,
AND THE FIRE PLACES WARM THE HOMES
AS STOCKINGS STUFFED WITH CARE,
WHEN THE CHRISTMAS MUSIC PLAYS OUR HEARTS
AND KINDER THOUGHTS PREVAIL,
A CHRISTMAS TREE, COLOURED LIGHTS TO SEE
WITH ALL OF SANTAS MAIL,
THE ISCICLES THAT HANG FROM TROUGH
AND FROSTY STANDING GUARD,
THE COOL WIND BLOWS AS WINTER SHOWS
IT STILL HAS ONE MORE CARD,
THE ROASTED TURKEY YET TO COME
WITH ALL THE SPECIAL TRIMS,
OUR FAMILY AND OUR FRIENDS UNITE
AND STREETS ARE FILLED WITH HYMNS,
AND AS WE GATHER QUIETLY ROUND
WITH OPEN HEARTS AND HANDS,
OUR THOUGHTS AND PRAYERS FOR ALL MANKIND
AND PEACE THROUGHOUT THE LANDS

House On A Hill

My DREAM IS TO HAVE A HOUSE ON A HILL
RIGHT BELOW THE EVENING SKY,
WHERE I COULD GLANCE THE NIGHTLY LIGHTS
AND FEEL THE BREEZE AND MOUNTAINS LIE,
AS VALLEYS SHINE
THEIR PUREST FUN,
AND SCENTS OF PASTURES,
ALL AS ONE,
WHERE COLOURED FLOWERS
SMILE IN RAY,
I HEAR THE PEACE
WHILE CHILDREN PLAY,
THE PATH THAT LEADS TO MY ABODE
PRESENTS THE FREEDOM TRAIL,
I SEALED THIS FIXTURE IN MY HEART
WITH HAMMER AND A NAIL,
AND AS DAWN BREAKS UPON THIS LAND
TOWARD ANOTHER DAY,
I LOOK OUT FROM WHERE I CAME
UP HIGH, ABOVE THE BAY

Inside The Crystal Falls

STANDING UNDER THE VIBRATING COOL FALLS
I REST
ARMS REACHED TO THE SKY
HEAD DOWN
GONE EVERY HARSH CRY,
GENTLE RUMBLING ON MY FINGER TIPS
FROZEN TIMES WHERE MOUNTAINS DRIP,
I DO REMEMBER YOU
I HAVE FALLEN FOR YOUR PAST BEAUTY
AND UNTO YOU
I SURELY KNOW
YOU ARE MY DUTY,
FOR HERE I ROAM A PLACE THAT SHOULD BE
FOR EVERY ACHE AND EVERY PLEA,
ROLLING THROUGH THE REALMS OF PEACE
TILL SEA HORSES FLY
TILL STARS BURN OUT
TILL AUTUMS FALL
AND ALL PAST PAIN CEASE,
INTO THE SOFT CLEAR BLUE PILLAR OF DREAMS.

Just A Memory

IF I COULD SEE ALL THE WONDERS OF THE WORLD
EVEN JOINED,
THEY COULD NOT SURPASS, YOU MY SPECIAL GIRL,
YOU RANK WHERE EAGLES BY
BEYOND THE DRIFTING SPACE, IMORTALS LIE,
NO EXPECTATIONS SAUGHT,
ONLY LOVING MEMORIES CAUGHT,
TOWARD OUR PRINCE PLANET WE FLOAT,
THE AIR IS SOFT, OUR TIME REMOTE,
TILL FOREVER GATES AND PASSAGES WE STAND
I TAKE YOUR HAND,
OUR SOULS BEGIN WITH TRUMPETS AT THE RISE
IN YOU, YOUR HEART, I FEEL YOUR EYES
PULSATING LIDS WITH CRAVING BIDS,
BE MY SHADOW AND I BE YOURS
AND SLEEP AWAY THE STARS WITH ME,
AS WE UNITE AND TEARS WILL ROLL
DRIFITING TO ETERNITY

Keeping Time

I HAVE HOPED UNTO THE MOUNTAINS
STARED AT THE SKYS FOR ANSWERS
AND THOUGHT AT MANY FOUNTAINS,
AND THE GIFT OF YOU
FROM A MUCH GREATER GOD
IN MY HEART, I KNOW TO BE TRUE.

Last Words

$\mathcal{A}$ few years ago, I responded to a call as a Police Officer in Toronto regarding a serious motor vehicle accident. On arrival at the scene, a female victim had been ejected from the vehicle and was lying on her back in the highway. Her injuries were so severe that I thought that there was a possibility that she may die. I could hear the ambulance close by. After administering basic First Aid to her, I knelt down beside her and she was softly calling out for her mother, who was not at the scene. I quickly ran up to a bystander in the crowd that had gathered and asked to use their cellular phone. I took the phone and knelt back down beside her and asked her for her mother's phone number and she softly gave me the number that was out of Province. I called the number, got her mother on the phone, said who I was and what had happened and held the phone up to the young ladies ear. I held her hand while she spoke. What this young lady said to her mother on the phone will forever be our secret. Her words brought tears to my eyes and changed me as a person forever. Through the excellent work of the Professional Doctors and Nurses at Centenary Hospital in Scarborough, Ontario, this young lady lived. I went to see her the following day at the hospital and she had her mother by her bedside and other family members. She started to cry when she saw me and gave me a big hug. A few weeks later, she sent my partner and I a very nice card which I will always treasure.

To this young lady, thank you for your words. You changed my life.

Little Or Fun

YOU GAVE ME LIFE
AND I STOOD THE TASK
THOUGH DARKENED SHEEP
I WORE NO MASK

TO SECRET WALLS
PROVIDE ME TOO
BEARING SCULPTURED WORDS
BUT DO AS I DO

FROM SEASONS CHANGE
TO REASONS NOT
MY MIND OF YOU
I ALWAYS SOUGHT

FROM HERE I AM
TO THERE I GO
SURELY GIFTS OF GOD
AT HARBOUR GROW

FOR I AM STRONG
MY JOURNEY COST
BUT HOLDING MY COURSE
I WAS NEVER LOST

Mangroves At Morgans Harbour

IN THE WARM SUNNY DAYS
I SAW THE RAYS THROUGH CRYSTAL WATERS,
PIERCING THE SHALLOW, TO THE MURK
SHADOWED COLOURED CORNERS ROAM
CLEAN FISH SWAY AT HOME,
ON THE BRANCHES
MUZZLE GRASP,
IN QUIET PLACES, SURELY LAUGH,
AND THROUGH THE RIVER LIKE PATHS SO SOFT,
I ROW ONE WITH NATURES NOISE,
THESE TREASURED TIMES
REPLACES TOYS,
MARINE TO SEE, THE SALTY WAND
LIKE MAGIC, A WHOLE NEW VIEW,
TWAS MY FREQUENT ROAM
I CALLED MY HOME,
I COULD MAKE MY MIND AT EASE
AND LAUGH AMONG
THE AIR AND TREES,
FOR I BUILT THE ATLANTIC
I RAFTED MANY STREAMS,
I FLEW LIKE A SEAGULL
AS I REHEARSED A THOUSAND DREAMS

Manta

I WAS PRIVILEDGED TO SWIM WITH YOU
WHEN I SPEARED THE REEFS OF OCHIO RIOS,
TO SEE ME, THEN TO ALLOW ME
WITH PURE CURTESY AND CURIOSITY,
YOUR WINGS THAT SPACED THE BLACK CORAL CLAN
WOULD BESTOW THE WATCH OF EVERY FAN,
SLOWLY AND SCARED AT FIRST
I HARDLY MOVE FOR FEAR THE WORST,
BUT YOU IN YOUR INWARD KIND
TEACHING
ITS TRUE PEACE I FIND,
GLIDING THROUGH YOUR REALM LIKE OWNING TIME
IT'S YOU AT PLAY, OR MAYBE DINE,
YOUR SLIGHT TOUCH OF MY SKIN IN FLOAT
BENEATH THE BUOYS, BENEATH THE BOAT,
A HUMBLING SMILE TO SAY THE MOST
AND I WILL REMEMBER THIS SEA AND COAST

Marching Home

NOW WE ARE TRULY FREE TO ROAM
LIKE KIN, BEYOND NO BOUNDS,
AS LAKES AND VALLEYS SLEEP THE TIME
BUT FOR ONLY LOVE ON COMMON GROUNDS,
WHERE PEACE IS SANCTIONED BY EVERY BREATH
AND FREE TO WORSHIP TILL TIME MARKS DEATH,
TILL HOMES ARE ALL A LOVING NEST
AND WELCOME SMILES WITH EVERY GUEST,
I DID MY BEST
NOW I CAN REST,
THE VALOR PUT TO STRENGTH, NOT YEILD
THE HUSH WIND BLOWS, THE KETTLE SOFT,
AS WE REMAKE THE PUNISHED PAST
AND PUT THE ANGERS OUT TO LOFT,
THOUGH WOUNDED, TIRED AND TROUBLED BE
OUR HEARTS STILL FROZEN IN THE TIME,
BRIGHT COLOUR OF THE TEARFUL TRUTH
THE ONLY FIERCE, THE ONLY SIGN,
COME DREAM AWAY THIS PEACE WITH ME
AND CLEAR THEIR EYES, THAT THEY MAY SEE,
AS KINGDOMS FAR AND WIDE DECREE
THE TIME MOVES ON
AND WE ARE FREE.

Men For Our Father

THROUGH MY EYES, YOU MAKE ME PROUD
I SEE YOU BOTH AS MEN,
YOU WALK AMONG THE THORNS OF LIFE
AND NEVER WOULD GIVE IN,
YOU CLIMB THE HILLS OF TOIL AND SWEAT
TO SHOW ME YOULL SUCCEED,
BACK DOWN YOU WON'T FROM ANY TASK
NO MATTER IF YOU BLEED,
THROUGH MY EYES IVE SEEN YOU'RE TEARS
THAT SHOW THAT YOU ARE STRONG,
THEY SHOW YOUR HEART IS KIND TO LOVE
BY SMILE AND DEED AND SONG,
AND THROUGH MY EYES I KNOW YOUR FAITH
BELIEVE, IN ANY WEATHER,
BACK TO BACK YOU FACE THE FOES
AND ALWAYS STICK TOGETHER,
AND THROUGH MY EYES I SEE YOUR FUTURES

THAT TEACH YOUR SONS AND DAUGHTERS,
YOU STICK TO LOVE
WITH HEART AND SOUL
AS TIME FLOWS LIKE THE WATERS,
AND THROUGH MY EYES I LOOK UP HIGH
A PLACE THAT WE WILL MEET,
ONE DAY WHEN LIFE RUNS OUT OF TIME
BEYOND THE DEEP OF DEEP,
REMEMBER THIS GOOD SONS OF MINE
MY HEART IS NEVER TORN,
FOR YOU MADE ME PROUD
MY BOYS, NOW MEN
THE DAY THAT YOU WERE BORN

My Olive Branch

WHEN I WAS SMALL, WITH ALL MY FRIENDS
AND PLAYED WITH SLIDES AND SWINGS,
WHEN I COULD RUN FOR MILES AT ONCE
LIKE ANGELS WITH THEIR WINGS,
I THOUGHT THAT I COULD LIVE FOREVER
AND MY DREAMS WOULD ALL COME TRUE,
BUT SOON I WATCHED MY TIME UNFOLD
AWAY FROM ME, TO YOU,
MY LAUGHTER SOON BECAME A SMILE
THAT GREW SOFTER WITH THE YEARS,
MY CHILDREN SOON BECAME MY LIFE
MY JOY WAS SHOWN WITH TEARS,
AS THE SEASONS CHANGED
AND TREES GREW BIG
MY THOUGHTS WERE NOT OF ME,
I WATCHED MY LOVED ONES, DO WHAT I,
BECAME MY DESTINY,

THE LONELY DAYS
OF FACING AGE
WITH WONDER AND OUR BELIEF,
BUT WISDOM BRINGS
AND MEMORIES SINGS
AND WARMS US IN OUR GRIEF,
MY LOVED ONES PASSED, I LOOKED TO GOD
I WAVE TO EVERY FRIEND,
WE WATCH THE WIND CARESS OUR TIME
AS WE SAIL TOWARD THE END,
THE DAY DRAWS NEAR WHEN WE SHALL MEET
AGAIN AS YOU DID TELL,
I HAVE SO MUCH TO SAY GRANDPA
WHEN TIME SOUNDS AT THE BELL.

My World Is Yours

IT DOES NOT LOOK LIKE I AM HERE
AND YOU SEE MY EYES, BUT NOT MY WORD,
I MOVE ALONG IN GENTLE TIME
THE OLD FAMILIAR VOICE NOT HEARD,
SO NOW YOU TAKE THE WHEEL MY CHILD
NOW YOU ARE TALL IN TIME,
YOU DECIDE MY FURTHERMORE
MY THOUGHTS NO LONGER MINE,
FOR NOW MY WORLDS NOT CLEAR TO ME
MY CHILD LIKE WAYS ARE YOURS TO CARE,
I ALWAYS HAVE YOU IN MY HEART
MY MIND IS FAR, BUT IM STILL HERE.

Northern Chill

EVEN WHEN THE FROST SETS IN
AND FLOWERS HIDE THEIR WORLDLY FACE,
I FIND TRANQUILITY ON THE RISE
MORE PLANTING OF THE SEEDS OF GRACE,
TURN SHARPLY TOWARD THE FLIGHT OF BIRDS
TO SEE WHERE WARMTH AND BRIGHTNESS TRY,
AS IF THE HUMID HAS REMORSE
WHILE SLEEPY SEASONS OFF TO BYE.

Ōgima

WE GET BY WITH EVERY TOIL AND TASK
WE STAND BY EACH ONE, WITHOUT AN ASK,
BE THERE FOR WHEN WE NEED US MOST
MY FRIENDS AND ME, I STAND TO TOAST

Pockets Of Love

I THOUGHT FOR A NIGHT AND DIDN'T GET SLEEP
I ROLLED IN MY BED AND GOT MAD,
BUT I FINALLY FOUND MY BIRTHDAY WISH
THIS IS WHAT I WILL SAY TO MY DAD:
"HAPPY BIRTHDAY DAD, YOU SURE ARE THE BEST
YOU MEAN MORE TO ME THAN THE EARTH,
I HAVE NOTHING TO GIVE
AND I HOPE YOU FORGIVE
BUT IVE LOVED YOU SO MUCH SINCE MY BIRTH,
I DON'T HAVE A JOB TO BUY YOU A GIFT
BUT I PROMISE TO ALWAYS BE GOOD,
AND A TIME WILL COME
WHEN ILL MAKE YOU PROUD
I WOULD DO IT RIGHT NOW IF I COULD,
YOU ALWAYS TAUGHT ME TO LOVE AND BE KIND
AND BE GRATEFUL FOR ALL FROM ABOVE,
YOUR GIFT IS NOT WRAPPED,
BUT IT'S WORTH MORE THAN GOLD
SO I BROUGHT YOU POCKETS OF LOVE"

Polar Power

THE SUBMERGED VIEW IS CLEAR
SWIMMING STROKES OF A POLAR BEAR

IN CHARGE, SLOW MOTION, CALM BUT STRONG
THE STROKES OF SPACELIKE WALKS ARE LONG

THE VISIONS LIKE MAGNETS TOWARD YOU
AMAZED BY WAY MORE THAN TWO

IN YOUR OWN SANCTITY OF EASE
TURN AGAIN AND GO, I PLEAD

YOU SHOW A STYLE OF OWNING WINGS
THROUGH THE WATER, WATCHING THINGS

Princess Wish

FOR IF I HAD A WISH FROM A PRINCES
A WISH SHE COULD GRANT, IF SHE MAY,
THE HEAVENS WOULD WELCOME MY ANSWER
OF BEING A POET FOR A DAY

River Ride

CRYSTAL BELLS AND ICE CREAM SHELLS
AND DIAMONDS SPARKLING LIGHT,
THE GOLDEN RAYS OF SUNSHINE
PURE TWINKLING STARS AT NIGHT,
HIBISCUS HILLS AND TANGERINE THRILLS
AND BIRCH OF ROLLING PLAINS,
SILVER SATIN, ROYAL CROWNS
WITH PEARLS THAT BRING THE FAMES,
THE SECRET SHADES OF ESCAPADES
THE WILD WIND RUNNING FREE,
AND GRAVITY PRESENTS NO MORE
SEE BIRDS FROM A TO Z,
I SLOWLY WAKE, I HESITATE
STILL FLOATING IN THE STREAM,
I BREATHE A SIGH, MY EYES TO SKY
TWAS ONLY JUST A DREAM

Rolling Tune

MY CHIN IS UP, MY EYES AHEAD
I OFTEN SMILE TOO MUCH,
MY CHILDHOOD DAYS IN MIXED UP WAYS
THEY NEVER WERE A CRUTCH,
I LOVE MY FRIENDS, FOR NO LOVE ENDS
JUST GRATEFUL FOR THE DAY,
GET OUT OF BED AND PUSH AHEAD
AS WITH MY HEART I LAY,
I SAT WITH KINGS AND PESANTS TOO
AND WALKED THE PATH OF PEACE,
WITH STRENGTH I FACE THE TASKS AT HAND
TILL SUN AND MOON DO CEASE,
THE MANY HURTS UPON MY MIND
AND SORROW I HAVE FELT,
I WILL NOT HIDE, I WALK WITH PRIDE
THESE CARDS WERE WHAT WAS DEALT,
AND WHILE I WORK THE FIELDS OF LIFE
WHERE DARK IS NOT TOO SOON,
IM GRATEFUL AS THE SECONDS ROLL
AS I WHISTLE ME A TUNE.

Seeing A Wish

TO SEE THE MORNING BIRDS IN SONG
TO MARVEL THE FLOWERS BLOOM FROM SEED,
THE OCEANS THAT LAUGH AND ROLL TOWARD THE SANDS
BUT IN MY WORLD, I SEE NO GREED

TO SEE THE FOODS THAT WE ARE BLESSED TO EAT
AND WATCH AS CHILDREN PLAY,
THE SUN UNCOVERS EVILS MIGHT
BUT IN MY WORLD, THERE IS NO DAY

TO WATCH A STREAM SLOWLY SWAYING BY
AS A DAY SEEMS TO MOVE ALONG,
THE DIFFERENT COLOURS THAT DEFINE OUR BEAUTY
CAN'T SEE, BUT I HEAR A SONG

I USED TO PRAY SO MY EYES COULD SEE
THE REASONS I COULD FIND,
THE PICTURES PAINT OF OTHER ONES
HAVE EYES BUT STILL ARE BLIND

Shadows And Embers

THOUGH THE FAIR SUN CASTS TRUE
I SEE NOT YOUR PRINT
BUT I SEE YOU

FOR TO BEHOLD IN HONEST FACE
IS TO SEE NOT WHAT OTHERS SEE
BUT TO BREATHE YOUR GRACE

THROUGH STREAMS THAT FLOW
PERFECT SILLOUTTES
ONLY THE ARTIST WOULD KNOW

FOR I AM THE GUEST OF YOU
WHAT HAS BEEN ETCHED
WHAT SHALL BE, ALWAYS TWO

Shandy

REFLECTING LIGHT IN COLOURS BEAM
YOU ARE THE BEAUTY, MAYBE QUEEN,
FOR IN MY VIEW YOU OPEN THOUGHTS
CREATIVE ON JUST MOVEMENT BE,
EVEN RAINBOWS CAST THEIR AWE
AND TINKLES TO THE NIGHT SO FREE,
YOU OVERLOOK WITH BOAST AND BRIGHT
DELIGHT THE SOULS THAT STARE,
THE RAYS OF LIGHT ACKNOWLEDGE YOU
EACH MOMENT YOU APPEAR,
SO SLEEP MY LOVE, PROVIDE OUR EYES
AND SING AN EVENING SONG,
THE NIGHT WIND BLOWS A SOFT REPLY
YOUR DIAMOND DAYS ARE LONG.

She Is Niagara

YOU ROLLING FORCE AGAINST THE SKY
THE BURSTING FOAMS OF WHITE,
FLOW TO THE EDGE,
A FALL TO GRACE
A ROAR WITH ALL YOUR MIGHT,
BUT YOU ARE GENTLE IN YOUR WAYS
THE WATER SPRAYS
IN SUNNY DAYS,
I FOUND A RAINBOW ALL COMPLETE
AGAINST YOUR BEAUTY LAY,
ANOTHER SIGHT
OF PURE DELIGHT
TO MAGNIFY YOU'RE DAY,
SO SURE TO GAZE, AS WE AMAZE
A GIFT FROM CLOUDS UP HIGH,
FOR YOU IMPRESS,
THE BIRDS THAT TEST
ABOVE HER, IN OPEN SKY,
YOU KNOW NO DAY, YOU MOVE IN TIME
SURE TO THE STROKE YOU BOAST,
AND THOSE THAT DARE
TO TEST THEIR FATES
IS WHEN SHE BREATHES THE MOST,
FOR SHE IS THERE TO GAZE UPON
SPECTACULAR FROM HER BIRTH,
ROLL ON MY LADY,
FALLS SO FREE
YOU WONDER OF THE EARTH

Sir Snowman

I ROLLED YOU UP INTO A MAN
AND NOW YOU'RE COLD AS ICE,
YOUR NOSE IS MADE OF CARROT STICKS
YOUR BLACK HATS FALLEN, TWICE
THE PIPE YOU SMOKE IS MADE OF WOOD
AND EYES ARE MADE OF NUTS,
AND WITH YOUR SCARF,
YOU HANDSOME MAN
AND THAT'S NO IF'S AND BUT'S,
THE BUTTONS ON YOUR COAT ARE BLACK
A BELT WITH BUCKLE TOO,
THE POLKA DOTS UPON YOUR CHEEKS
A GIFT FROM ME, TO YOU,
I PUT YOU ON A HILL TO SEE
THE CHILDREN WHILE AT PLAY,
YOU REALLY MAKE THIS SPECIAL TIME
A MR SNOWMAN DAY

Solo Flight

YOU NEVER WATCHED ME GROW
INTO ALL YOU HAD THOUGHT IT SHOULD BE,
BUT I SURFED WITH THE EVERGREENS
I TO THEM AND THEY TO ME.

Sugar Man Brooks

I ADMIRE YOU AS YOU SWING YOUR CUTLASS
AND CUT THE SUGAR CANE,
I SEE YOU SWEAT, I PLACE MY BET
IT'S ALL A WORKING GAME,
I HEAR YOU SING OF TIMES GONE BY
THAT GIVES YOU STRENGTH TO TOIL,
BUT I RESPECT YOU BROTHER MAN
AS YOU WORK THIS SACRED SOIL,
YOU STOP TO TAKE A DRINK OF RUM
AND SMILE AS IT GOES DOWN,
YOU KEEP YOUR SMILE AND LOOK AT ME
THEN BACK TO CUTTING DOWN,
YOUR BIG AND STRONG MR SUGAR MAN
A STICK WITH HOOK IN HAND,
BLESS ALL YOUR WORK AND FAMILY
FOR YOU HAVE BUILT THIS LAND.

The Bricks I Lay

WHEN THE LIGHTS OF LIFE APPEAR TO DIM
AND THE DUST BEGINS TO CLEAR,
THE CHILDREN GROWN, MORE ANSWERS KNOWN
AND TIME BEGINS TO WEAR,
WHEN THE WEATHERED SKIN SOON SETTLES IN
AND HUMILITY TAKES ITS PLACE,
THE WONDERS OF OUR TIME CAN TELL
WERE HERE BY ONLY GRACE,
WHEN LIFE DESIRES ALL SOON EXPIRES
AND WE ARE LEFT TO TEST,
THE ONLY QUESTION LEFT TO ASK
IS DID WE DO OUR BEST,
OUR YOUTHFULNESS HAS TRADED US
AND NOW IT'S WAIT AND SEE,
IT'S WHAT WE DID, WHILE OTHERS LIVE
CREATE OUR DESTINY,
AND WHEN I LAY BACK IN MY FINAL REST
AS THROUGH MY LIFE I SIFT,
WHERE ASHES JOIN AND DUST UNITES
I'LL SAY THIS WAS A GIFT

The Brightest Stars

WHAT HIDDEN VIRTUES MAY BE
FOR THOSE WITH BROKEN WING,
A VOICE TO SPEAK
FOR THOSE THAT SEEK
AS THEY FLY IN HOPE TO SING.

This Castle I Dream

THOUGH IM STANDING THERE, COULD ALMOST TOUCH
MY DREAMS ARE LOST IN SONG,
ALTHOUGH THE TIMED TINKER FLIES
MY JOURNEY TO IMAGINE LONG,
CAPTURING CREATIVITY
IMAGINATIONS CLOCK,
A LITTLE MOUSE THAT STARTED IT
THE FAIRY TALE, TICK TOCK, TICK TOCK,
AROUND THE GLOBE, FAR FETCHED IT TELLS
BUT ALTERING EVERY AND ALL,
THE SONGS ARISE, SEE OLDER CRY
WE FEEL THE WORLD IS SMALL,
SO CARRY ME TO THE PERHAPS SO
AS I JOIN THE YOUNG AT HEART,
SOMETIMES THERE HAS TO BE A PLACE
MYSTERIOUS DREAMS OF COLOURED ART.

Tiki Lullabye

COOL MIST, EXOTIC BLISS
TROPICAL BIRDS OF ALL SHADES OF BLOOM,
SINGING VOICES THAT TWEET WORLDS
UP THERE WITH THAT DISTANT MOON,
THEY SING ABOUT LIFE, IN PARADISE
A SMILE THAT PULLS TEARS FROM AIR,
SWINGING AND DANCING TO TREES TUNES
IS ALL MY BEATING HEART COULD BEAR,
BAMBOO CRIES, WATERFALL EYES
MORE SONGS OF FOREST GLEE,
I SEPARATE MY DREAMS AND THOUGHTS
IT'S STILL MY ALWAYS REALITY,
OH TAKE ME TO THAT PLACE AWAY
WHERE FURTHER SPACE MEETS SKY,
AND LET ME SLEEP THE HOLLOW SOUNDS
INSIDE MY TIKI LULLABYE.

Till A Kiss

WITH THIS KISS OF LOVE
I SEAL OUR TIMELESS BOND
WITH YOU TO TOMORROWS NEVER,
WHATEVER RESTING PLACE WHERE WE SHALL JOIN,
IT WILL ALWAYS BE AS ONE
FOR THE SCENTED JUDES AND SAIL WINDS
OF WHICH OUR HANDS WERE JOINED,
AND QUIET MOMENTS OF SMILES,
FUSED WITH PROMISED STARES,
VISIONED WITH FRESH MIST AND TOGETHER PASTURES,
I FEEL YOUR SOFTNESS,
AS MY TEARS EMBRACE YOUR TENDER BEING,
WE WILL UNITE IN WHERE WE SPOKE,
AND I WILL NOT SLEEP IN COMFORT TILL YOU LAND
ON SUNNY BEACHES
WITH SILKEN SAND,
WITH THIS KISS, STROKED WITH YOUR
SLIGHT WARM BREATH
I SECURE, EACH AND EVERY OF YOUR LOVES,
AS I FEEL OUR BEATING HEARTS
POUNDING PATHS OF SNOW LIKE DOVES.

Till Forever

AS CIRCLED SOFT CLOUDS THAT FLOAT IN PEACE
I GIVE TO YOU MY HEART,
THE PROMISE OF MY LOVE FOR YOU
WILL LAST
TILL TIME DOES PART,
I FEEL YOUR TEARS UPON MY LIFE
AS IN YOUR EYES I SEE,
THAT SUNS WILL RISE
IN MANY SKIES
AND CREATE OUR DESTINY,
SO TAKE MY HAND, MY EVER ONE
AS TOGETHER WE WILL FLY,
LIKE FLOWERS IN AN OPEN FIELD
THAT FACE THE OPEN SKY,
AND AS I STAND TO TAKE MY VOW
I PROMISE AS A MAN,
TO LOVE, PROTECT AND HONOUR YOU
IN EVERY WAY I CAN.

Till

M Y ONE THAT I ADORE.
IN WHOM I BUILD MY LOVE SURROUND
A SMILE, A CHEERFUL STEP OF SOUND,
CASTS EVERY SOFT BREATH TO MY TEST
FOR SHE IS ALL OUR WORLD TO NEST,
YOU'RE EYES THEY DRAW MY FLOATING PULSE
TOWARD A WIND OF FATE I NEVER DREAMED,
THAT PROCLAIMS INVINCIBLY,
IT WAS WRITTEN,
IT ALWAYS SEEMED,
PROVIDING ALL THAT WE AMAZE,
IN SUNNY DAYS, OR OTHER DAYS,
MY SWEET, MY SUMMER SKY AND EVENING HAZE
WHAT ARE THE TIMES,
THERE ONLY DAYS,
WE WILL WALK IN THAT FOREVER RAY TO GATES AFAR
AND I WILL CRY OUT YOUR NAME UNTIL
I FIND MY NOTHERN STAR,
TWO TONES OF THE MUSIC OF THE EARTH,
AND WE WERE MEANT
BEFORE OUR BIRTH.

Unto A Farmer

I REST MY TRUST THROUGH MANY DAYS
UPON THIS SACRED FIELD,
MY PLOUGH HAS WORKED THE FRESH SOFT EARTH
WHATEVER IT MAY YIELD,
IN SILENCE AS THE DAY GOES BY
JUST ME ALL DRESSED IN SWEAT,
THE LONGER DAYS WITH HOTTER RAYS
I PUT IN ALL I GET,
I SOOTHE THE LAND IN MY OWN WAY
SO GRATEFUL FOR THE TOIL,
THE RAIN WILL COME TO NURTURE US
AND GIVE LIFE TO THE SOIL,
I LEAVE THE FIELDS WHEN SUN GOES DOWN
AND LAY BACK IN MY CHAIR,
I STARE ACROSS THE MOONLIT EVE
GOD BLESS THE CROPS WE BARE

Water Dolls

FOLLOWING THE BOAT TOWARD THE SEAS
MY FRIENDS ESCORT WITH PLAY,
I LEAN TOWARD THE WATERS SPLASH
AND MEET HER EYES TO SAY,
I HAVE YOU IN MY HEART MY FRIEND
WISH WE COULD SWIM TOGETHER,
SHES WAVING FIN, MY MIND GOES DIM
THIS WARM AND SUNNY WEATHER,
SHE MAKES A SOUND AS IF TO SAY
COME SPLASH WITH ME, COME LAUGH AND PLAY,
ITS ME AND HER AND WATCHFUL EYE
SHE REALLY SETS OUR COURSE,
A FRIEND TO ME, A BEAUTY SEE
LET EVERY HEART ENDORSE,
A ROLL A SPLASH, A DIVE A DASH
AND BUBBLES ALL ABOUT,
A POWER TAIL THAT BEATS THE SAIL
AND GENTLE MIST FROM SPOUT,
GOODBYE MY FRIEND, UNTIL WE MEET
I FEEL YOUR COMFORT STILL,
IN DIFFERENT WATERS WE SHALL MEET
WHEN THERES A WAY AND WILL.

Waving Goodbye

In my vision, I see your tale
though darkness presumes to be
you will not fail,
for greater powers shine you're light
though tabled by black stormy days
you will prevail night after night,
though fallen rocks
all crumbled after,
surely you will reveal
anger turned to laughter,
time besets all stages
always in tune
as we turn lifes pages,

FOR TO BE, IS TO LEARN
AND TO TROD THE COBLESTONES OF HUMANITY
IS TO HEAL LIKE AGED FERN,
AMID THE FROST
ONE WAY ONLY
NOTHING LOST,
VIRTUES OF A MAN
RISING WITH THE SUN
I KNOW YOU CAN.

Where Angels Sleep

I SEE THE PLACE WHERE FONDNESS LAY
AS MARBLE STANDS THE TEST OF TIME,
TRUE TO THOSE WHO CHERRISH THOUGHTS
AWAIT THE ANSWERS OF MANKIND,
THE FLOWERS TELL
THE CHANGING DAYS,
AS SEASONS SHOW
HER ANGLED WAYS,
AND PEACE PERFORMS ON AGELESS STAGE

I HEAR THE BATTLES, SOONER SOFT,
THE BIRDS THAT CHORUS NATURES HYMNS
SOON LOST BEYOND THE CRYSTAL FROST,
AND WE SHALL BE
AS PROMISED THEN,
WHERE GARDENS GROW
FOREVER BLISS,
ONE LAST MOMENT
WITH OUR LOVE,
ONE LAST ROSE
AND ONE LAST KISS.

Wonder Colours

MAYBE YOU LIKE GREEN AND GOLD
AND I LIKE BLUE AND BLACK,
OR WATER COLOURS CANVAS CLAD
WITH PALLETS IN A PACK,
THE OILY PAINTS WITH SLIGHTLY TAINTS
CREATING LOADS OF SWIRLS,
AND OCEANS SENDING FROM THE DEEP
THEIR SATIN PRECIOUS PEARLS,
BUT I LIKE WONDER COLOURS THAT
CAN BRIGHTEN UP THE SUN,
AND MOVE THE WORLD IN TONES OF PEACE
AND BLEND US ALL AS ONE

Letter to Miss Reid, Toronto Children's Aid Society, circa 1959.

Date: 2014.

Dear Miss Reid

Just to let you know, I arrived safely.
Thank you for being so kind to me and always taking me out for fish and chips
and giving me my winter coat and winter hat.

Kenny Miller
Former Crown Ward
Now: Kenny Lord

Our Children, Our Care, Their Right

Author Kenny Lord
Also Author of, "On Faith We Fly"—Poetry by Nature.

About The Author

This is the second book of Poetry by Author Kenny Lord. The first book, "On Faith We Fly" was published in 2013 by Authorhouse Publishing.

Kenny is still a Police Officer with the Toronto Police Service and as an Author, is currently working on his third book of Poetry. He lives in Whitby, Ontario, Canada, is married to his amazing wife, Tisha and is the father of three adult children, Taylor, Steven and Kaitlin.

Kenny's first book, "On Faith We Fly" was a collection of Poetry that he has written over the years since he was a young child growing up in Jamaica. This second book, "The Bells Of Humility" was written within the last year. It is a collection of various topics of Poetry, mixed with Love, Humour, reality and fiction.

One of Kenny's favourite phrases is, "There's a little bit of Disney in everyone". He has been to Disney World many times and it is his favourite fun filled place to visit. Enjoy the dreams of this Poetry, the magic and excitement that goes with it, the worlds that we don't see sometimes, but are there when we need them to be. The laughter and the smiles.

Thanks Walt. You're the best!

Author - Kenny Lord